Hávamál

The
Sayings
of the
Vikings

Hávamál

The
Sayings
of the
Vikings

Translated from the
Original by
Björn Jónasson

GUDRUN

GUDRUN publishing
Reykjavík – Göteborg – Oslo

The Sayings of the Vikings © GUDRUN 1992
6. impression 1995
English translation © Björn Jónasson 1992
Foreword © Matthías Viðar Sæmundsson 1992
Translation of Foreword © Bernard Scudder 1992
Cover Design: Björn Jónasson and Helgi Hilmarsson

ISBN 9979-9070-0-2 (Hard cover)
ISBN 9979-9070-1-0 (Paperback)

Palatino 10 - 12p and Goudy 14p
Recycled paper

Printed in Iceland
by Oddi Ltd. Printing Press

Table of contents

Introduction

Hávamál is one of the more famous and certainly one of the most popular of the so-called Eddaic poems. The part of Hávamál which is published here is unique among the Eddaic poems in its being neither heroic nor mythological, but rather a poem of didactic nature.

The Eddas signify for the northern culture what the Vedas mean to India and the Homeric poems are for the Greeks. Their variety and wealth are such, that they have been a source of inspiration and delight for generations, and still are.

Scholars do not agree on where the Hávamál was written, nor when; some argue it originated in Norway, some hold it was composed in Iceland, others still in the British Isles. Apart from the problem of discovering where the Hávamál was composed, there is the question of origination. Is it a collection of ancient sayings, which were hovering in the cultural atmosphere of the ancestors of the Vikings, and finally written down by a scribe in one of these countries? Is it a mixture of Latin proverbs and the old heathen wisdom bound together in the metre of the Edda?

The question of age of the Hávamál is of course related to the questions of where and how. There is almost a consensus that it was composed in the period around AD700-900, though it could have been written down for the first time later.

One thing is certain, however. The spirit of the poem, at least, has been greatly influenced by the attitude and culture of the Viking era culminating in the period AD800-1000.

The aim of this book is to make the Hávamál accessible to the English reading public. Many people have helped me greatly. I would like to thank Mr. Christopher Sanders of the Arnamagnæan Institute in Copenhagen and Mr. Martin Regal of the University of Iceland, for their invaluable criticism, and especially Mr. Bernard Scudder for his criticism, ideas and inspiration. Where this translation has succeeded, it is because of the aid of these generous people, and where it has failed, it is through faults of mine. Finally I would like to thank Mr. Don Brandt for proofreading and, last but not least, my family and friends for their support.

Björn Jónasson

Foreword

The Vikings and their descendants lived in a world where Christianity had difficulty in establishing its relevance to their everyday lives in the far north. For this reason, the heathen philosophy of life lived on in the minds of the people for centuries after it was officially replaced; knowledge of times of old was handed down from one generation to the next in various ways, despite widespread attempts to suppress it.

The Wisdom of the North, Hávamál, grants us insights into the heathen world that remain timeless. Although more than a thousand years old, this poetry could have been written yesterday. Much of it seems incapable of becoming outdated, since in important respects man himself has hardly changed in the course of the centuries. The essential qualities of life, too, are still the same as they were in the day that the Hávamál was written: A man who has fire, a view of the sun, good health and personal integrity is better placed than one whose life is spent in pursuit of wealth, of luxury and of impressing others. Nothing can take such a man´s life away, for although death is inescapable, his posthumous reputation will never die.

Heathen culture in the north had a tenacity that the Mediterranean dialectics of good and evil, of this world and the next, could not overcome for many centuries, perhaps not until the eighteenth century. Until then, pagan belief lived alongside or beneath official worship, threatening it in various ways. It was common, for example, for seventeenth-century sorcerors to invoke the divine powers of heathendom – Odin, Thor and Frey – and fire worship still persisted. Unlike most other places, the Church in Iceland and Scandinavia did not manage to establish Christian attitudes as a common social foundation until they had been practised for many centuries, and even then it remained fragile.

The ethics of the Hávamál are above all rooted in belief in the value of the individual, who is nonetheless not alone in the world but tied by inextricable bonds to nature and society; to adherents of such a philosophy, the cycle of life was single and indivisible, the living world in all its manifestations formed a harmonious whole. Infringements upon nature struck at the root of a man´s own existence. In the old philosophy of the North, each individual was responsible for his own life, shaped his own fortune or misfortune and created a life for himself from his own resources.

Perhaps the heathen philosophy of life has never had a more immediate message than today, in this age that practises contempt for humanity and nature, instead of admiration.

Matthías Viðar Sæmundsson
Senior Lecturer in Icelandic Literature,
University of Iceland

Hávamál

Advice to a Visitor

When passing
a door-post,
watch as you walk on,
inspect as you enter.
It is uncertain
where enemies lurk
or crouch in a dark corner.

How to Seat a Guest

Giver of the feast!
Your guest is here.
Where shall he sit?
Fast temper grows
in a far seat.
Prompt him not to prove
                    his mettle.

Hospitality

The newcomer
needs fire
his knees are numb.
A man who has made
his way over mountains
needs food and fresh linen.

Courtesy

A guest needs
giving water
fine towels and friendliness.
A cheerful word
a chance to speak
kindness and concern.

Worldliness

The traveller must
train his wits.
All is easy at home.
He who knows little
is a laughing-stock
amongst men of the world.

Attending a Feast

No man should call
himself clever
but manage his mind.
A sage visitor
is a silent guest.
The cautious evades evil.
Never a friend
more faithful,
nor greater wealth, than
                        wisdom.

Seeking Knowledge

The cautious guest
who comes to the table
speaks sparingly.
Listens with ears
learns with eyes.
Such is the seeker of
              knowledge.

Independence

It is fortunate
to be favoured
with praise and popularity.
It is dire luck
to be dependent
on the feelings of a fellow-
man.

Opinion of Others

He is fortunate
who is favoured
with respect and good reason.
Advice given
by others
is often ill counsel.

Wisdom

Better weight
than wisdom
a traveller cannot carry.
The poor man´s strength
in a strange place,
worth more than wealth.

Alertness

Better weight
than wisdom
a traveller cannot carry.
A clear head
is good company.
Drink is a dangerous friend.

Drinking

Ale
has too often
been praised by poets.
The longer you drink
the less sense
your mind makes of things.

Responsibility

A king´s son should be
               thoughtful
thorough and silent
brave in battle.
A man should be happy
and in good humour
to his dying day.

Self-Deceit

Only fools
hope to live forever
by escaping enemies.
Age promises
no peace
though the spear spares them.

Bad Manners

At a feast
the fool chatters
or he stares and stammers.
Just as soon as
his jug is full
ale unveils his mind.

Experience

He is truly wise
who´s travelled far
and knows the ways of the
                              world.
He who has travelled
can tell what spirit
governs the men he meets.

Good Manners

A man should drink
in moderation
be sensible or silent.
None will find
fault with your manners
though you retire
          in good time.

Self-Discipline

The glutton does not
guard himself
eats till he's ill.
Wiser men
only mock
a fool's fat belly.

Moderation

The cattle know
when to come home
from the grazing ground.
A man of lean wisdom
will never learn
what his stomach can store.

Happiness

He is unhappy
and ill-tempered
who meets all with mockery.
What he doesn´t know,
but needs to,
are his own familiar faults.

Worry

The unwise man
is awake all night
worries over and again.
When morning rises
he is restless still,
his burden as before.

Face Value

The unwise man
assumes that only
friends laugh to his face.
At the table with the wise
he cannot tell
what they say behind
                         his back.

The Dangers of Naivety

The unwise man
imagines
a smiling face, a friend.
Surprised to find
how little support
he musters at a meeting.

False Security

A fool thinks
he´s full of wisdom
when he´s safe and sound.
When alone
he is at a loss
for courage and cunning.

When to Keep Silent

Often it´s best
for the unwise man
to sit in silence.
His ignorance
goes unnoticed
unless he tells too much.
It´s the ill fortune
of unwise men
that they cannot keep silent.

The Nature of Gossip

The inquisitive man
appears clever,
if he can ask and answer well.
Gossip, thus,
gathers speed,
cannot be kept still.

Talking Too Much

Much nonsense
a man utters
who talks without tiring.
A ready tongue
unrestrained
brings bad reward.

How to Treat a Fellow

Do not ever
mock other
men at a meeting.
They pass for wise
who pass unnoticed
stay dry in the storm.

How to
Avoid Making Enemies

It makes sense
to set off home
when guest mocks guest.
Who can tell
at the table
if he laughs with angry men?

Quarrels

Friends often
fight with words
when together at the table.
Feuds always
follow
when guests goad each other.

When and How to Eat

Always rise
to an early meal,
but eat your fill before a feast.
If you´re hungry
you have no time
to talk at the table.

The Nature of Friendship

A bad friend
is far away
though his cottage is close.
To a true friend
lies a trodden road
though his farm lies far away.

How to Preserve Friendship

Go you must.
No guest shall stay
in one place for ever.
Love will be lost
if you sit too long
at a friend´s fire.

A Home Is a Castle

Better a humble
house than none.
A man is master at home.
A pair of goats
and a patched roof
are better than begging.

Poverty

Better a humble
house than none.
A man is master at home.
A beggar has
a bleeding heart
where every meal is alms.

Caution

Never walk
away from home
ahead of your axe and sword.
You can´t feel a battle
in your bones
or foresee a fight.

Generosity

None is so just
and generous
as not to gladden at a gift.
None so abstinent
or open-handed
to refuse a just reward.

Financial Sense

Become not
a beggar
to the money you make.
What´s saved for a friend
a foe may take.
Good plans often go awry.

Lasting Friendship

Give each other
good clothes
as friends for all to see.
To give and take
is a guarantee
of lasting love.

How to Be Cunning

Be your friend´s
true friend.
Return gift for gift.
Repay laughter
with laughter again
but betrayal with treachery.

Beware of Enemies

Be your friend´s
true friend
to him and his friends.
Beware
of befriending
an enemy´s friend.

How to Cultivate Friendship

A true friend
whom you trust well
and wish for his good will:
Go to him often
exchange gifts
and keep him company.

How to Treat False Friends

If you have a friend
whom you hardly trust
but wish for his good will:
Be fair in speech
but false in thought
return betrayal with
                    treachery.

Dissimulation

You have a friend
you hardly trust
in whom you cannot confide,
with fair smiles
and false words
repay cunning in kind.

Solitude and Company

When I was young
and walked alone,
alone I lost my way.
I felt rich
when I found company.
Man delights in man.

Prosperity

The brave and generous
have the best lives.
They´re seldom sorry.
The unwise man
is always worried,
fears favours to repay.

The Importance
of Appearances

Two wooden stakes
stood in the field,
there I hung my hat
           and cloak.
They had character
in fine clothes.
Naked I was nothing.

Loneliness

A lone fir
in an open field
withers away.
A lone man
loved by none
how can he live long?

False Peace

False peace
with bad friends
burns faster than fire.
In a few days
the flame goes out
all love is lost.

Extravagance

Load no man
with lavish gifts.
Small presents often win
                 great praise.
With a loaf cut
and a cup shared
I found fellowship.

Spiritual Grandeur

Of small sands
of small seas
small minds are made.
Not all men
are matched in wisdom
the imperfect are easy to find.

Moderation and Prosperity

Moderately wise
a man should be
not too crafty or clever.
The best of lives
is led by those
who know the measure of
                    many things.

Moderation and Happiness

Moderately wise
a man should be
not too crafty or clever.
A learned man's heart
whose learning is deep
seldom sings with joy.

To Know One´s Fate

Moderately wise
a man should be
not too crafty and clever.
A man´s fate
should be firmly hidden
to preserve his peace of mind.

Shyness

A log´s flame
leaps to another
fire kindles fire.
A man listens
thus he learns.
The shy stays shallow.

The Early Bird . . .

Wake early
if you want
another man´s life or land.
No lamb
for the lazy wolf.
No battle´s won in bed.

Agility

Rise early
attend to work
if there´s no helping hand.
The morning sleeper
has much undone.
The quick will catch the prize.

Foresight

A man should know
how many logs
stubs and strips of bark
to collect in summer
to keep in stock
wood for his winter fires.

Pride and Prejudice

Eat well
when you´re off to a visit
be clean though your clothes
                        are poor.
Be not ashamed
of your shoes and socks
still less of the horse you have.

How Not to Behave

Spying and prying
the predator eagle
approaches the ocean.
So is a man
at a meeting
who is favoured by few.

The Nature of Secrecy

Ask you must
and answer well
to be called clever.
One may know your secret
never a second.
If three, a thousand will
                        know.

The Use of Power

A prudent man
wields his power
in modest measure.
With brave men he finds
that none is foremost
or excels in all things.

The Unwelcome Guest

To many a place
I made my way late,
and far too soon to some.
The ale was drunk
or yet unserved
the unwelcome guest is
                untimely.

The Nature of Hospitality

I would be invited
everywhere
if I needn´t eat at all.
Or if I left two hams
at the house of a friend
where I´ve eaten only one.

The Basics of Life

A man needs warmth,
the warmth of fire
and of the shining sun.
A healthy man
is a happy man
who´s neither ill nor injured.

Look on the Bright Side

Though your health is ailing
all is not lost
your sons can swell your pride
your brave kinsmen
your fine cattle
your work well done.

Poor – but Alive ...

It is better to live
than lie dead.
A dead man gathers no
                    goods.
I saw warm fire
at a wealthy man´s house
himself dead at the door.

Everyone Has His Use

The lame rides a horse
the maimed drives the herd
the deaf is brave in battle.
A man is better
blind than buried.
A dead man is deft at
                    nothing.

Do Not Be Governed
by Money

Money often
makes an ape
of many a good man.
Some are wealthy
others want.
Meagre means are no shame.

Keeping Your Name Alive

A son is better
though late begotten
of an old and ailing father.
Only your kin
will proudly carve
a memorial at the main gate.

Renown

Cattle die
kinsmen die
all men are mortal.
Words of praise
will never perish
nor a noble name.

About the title

The title of this collection of poetic proverbs in the original is Hávamál, which means literally the Words of the High One. The High One is Odin (or Woden), the foremost of the Norse gods. Odin is the Northern equivalent to the Greek Zeus and the Roman Jupiter.

In Hávamál, or the Words of the High One, the god gives advice to us mortals on how to behave and manage in order to lead a prosperous and worthy life.

The title of this English version, The Sayings of the Vikings, refers to the fact that this poem is perhaps the purest example of the ethics of the Vikings, of all the literature of the Viking era. This poem with its pearls of shrewd wisdom, of terse humour and of noble sentiment is the kernel of the spirit of the Vikings.

The Metre of Hávamál

The Hávamál is written in a metre called Ljóðaháttur, which means literally Poetic Metre, indicating a certain seniority among the metres of old times.

The stanza of ljóðaháttur contains typically six lines or two units of three lines each. The first two lines in each unit are tied together by alliteration, and the third is also decorated with alliteration.

What is alliteration? Alliteration means that a vowel or a consonant of a stressed syllable is echoed by repeating the same consonant or vowel (in alliteration, any two vowels alliterate).

For example:

1. Better a humble

2. house than none.

3. A man is master at home.

4. A pair of goats

5. and a patched roof

6. are better than begging.

The first two lines in each unit (1 & 2 and
4 & 5, respectively) have two stresses, while
the last line (3 and 6 resp.) has two to four
stresses.

For example:

1. Better a humble

2. house than none.

3. A man is master at home.

4. A pair of goats

5. and a patched roof

6. are better than begging.

The reader can best realize the effect of
Hávamál by reciting it aloud. The melody
and rhythm arise not just from the allitera-
tive echoes, but from the contrast of the
alliterating and non-alliterating stressed
sounds. To quote Charles W. Dunn, of
Harvard University: "The ear is constantly
affected by the unpredictable alternations of
similarities and dissimilarities; and, because
of the freedom of the syllabic count, the
placement of the beat in each half-line is also
unpredictably varied. One can train oneself
to hear such music; and music it is."